CIVIL AIRCRAFT IN COLOUR

Hiroshi Seo

First published in 1984 by
Yami-kei Publishers Co. Ltd. Tokyo, Japan

Photographs © Hiroshi Seo, 1984

Text © Jane's Publishing Company Limited 1985

First published in the United Kingdom
in 1985 by Jane's Publishing Company Limited
238 City Road, London EC1V 2PU

ISBN 0 7106 0346 0

Distributed in the Philippines
and the USA and its dependencies by
Jane's Publishing Inc
135 West 50th Street
New York, NY 10020

Printed in Japan

JANE'S

Contents

Boeing 747   The world's largest passenger aircraft, known by its popular name of 'Jumbo', first flew on 9 February 1969, and commenced commercial service in January, 1970.

The 747 cruises at a speed almost as fast as its four-engined long-range predecessors but its wide-body fuselage has more than doubled the passenger capacity, enabling considerable reduction of the operating cost per passenger. It plays the star role in international commercial aviation.

JAL Boeing 747-300, operating non-stop between Tokyo and Los Angeles. Narita New Tokyo International Airport, August 1984.

Boeing 747 One of the Jumbo's characteristics is its double-decked nose section, the cockpit being positioned on the upper level, with a passenger cabin behind it. The latest version 747-300 has an extended floor in this upper-deck cabin accommodating up to 85 passengers.

Philippine Airlines Boeing 747-200B taking off from Honolulu Airport, May 1982.

Boeing 747 The Jumbo can be seen in several versions. The basic type is the 747-100, followed by the -200B with increased range performance, while the more recent -300 series feature an extended upper deck passenger cabin. Other variants include the 747-200F exclusive freight carrier, the -200C passenger/freight convertible, and the -200B Combi for mixed passenger and freight operations. Special modifications are the 747SR short-range version and the 747SP shorter-bodied derivative of the 747-100B for extreme range operations over lower density routes. Production of the 747 has already surpassed the 600 mark, with more orders still coming in. At present, no comparable development plans exist among any of Boeing's competitors, and it seems certain that the 747 will remain dominant in this super-size airliner category. The earlier versions will probably be replaced by an advanced 'stretched' model of the 747, expected to appear in the near future.

Opposite page, above left: *ANA's Boeing 747SR seating 500 passengers is specially designed for short-haul operations. Haneda Airport, October 1984.*

Below left: *Boeing 747-100 of Virgin Airlines, a British low-fare trans-Atlantic operator. London Gatwick Airport, September 1984.*

Above right: *Boeing 747-200F of Flying Tigers, an American freight service company. Narita Airport, August 1984.*

Centre: *Boeing 747-100 of United Airlines, the largest airline operator in the USA. Narita Airport, August 1984.*

Below right: *Boeing 747-200B of CP Air, Canada, a trans-Pacific operator. Narita Airport, August 1983.*

This page, above left: *Boeing 747-300 of KLM Royal Dutch Airlines, whose origin dates back to 1920. Narita Airport, August 1983.*

Above right: *Pan American World Airways Boeing 747SP. A Pan Am 747SP made the first non-stop flight between Tokyo and New York. Narita Airport, August 1984.*

Below: *CACC-China's Boeing 747SP used for long-range international transport. Narita Airport, August 1983.*

Ilyushin Il-86 The Soviet Union's first wide-bodied jetliner, the Il-86 made its maiden flight in December 1976. It is equivalent in size to the DC-10 but is powered by four engines, and its limited range may account for the relatively small number of Il-86s in use. However, an improved version designated Il-96, when completed, could be the main Soviet carrier in this category.

Ilyushin Il-86 of Soviet Union's flag carrier Aeroflot, the world's largest airline operator. Farnborough Air Show, September 1984.

McDonnell Douglas DC-10 A wide-bodied trijet developed for medium-haul operations, the initial model DC-10-10 was first flown in August 1970 and followed soon afterwards by the -30 and -40 long-range versions, securing a place in the market ahead of its rival Lockheed L-1011. After evaluation, the US Air Force also adopted the DC-10 for aerial refuelling and transport duties. The total production is now close to 400 aircraft.
DC-10-10 of Western Airlines, operating mainly in the western part of the USA. Los Angeles Airport, May 1982.

DC-10   The long-range versions of the DC-10, Series -30 and -40, feature increased fuel capacity, broadened centre wing section and an additional undercarriage unit below the centre fuselage. Other variants include the -30CF passenger/cargo convertible model and the -30F freight carrier.

Left: *Ghana Airways DC-10-30, London Heathrow Airport, September 1984.*

Above left: *DC-10-30, the first wide-body jetliner of Bangladesh Biman, Heathrow Airport, September 1984.*

Above right: *Passenger/cargo convertible DC-10-30CF of World Airways, USA. Los Angeles Airport, March 1984.*

Below left: *JAL's international carrier DC-10-40. Domestic service DC-10s have no additional dual-wheel bogie unit under the fuselage centreline. Narita Airport, August 1983.*

Below right: *DC-10-30 of Indianapolis-based American Trans Air. Gatwick Airport, September 1984.*

DC-10 The upswing of twin-engined jets such as the Boeing 767, Airbus A300 and A310, has cast a shadow over the wide-bodied trijet aircraft represented by the DC-10 which are less in demand. To reverse this declining situation, McDonnell Douglas plans to develop an improved version known as MD-11X.

DC-10-30 of VIASA Venezuelan International Airways. Miami Airport, March 1984.

Lockheed L-1011 TriStar DC-10's rival in terms of a wide-body of equivalent size, the L-1011 medium-range trijet suffered from lack of expected sales, resulting in the discontinuation of production in August 1983, 13 years after its debut. The total output numbered 248 aircraft. The TriStar is known to have incorporated more advanced technological features than the DC-10, but the disappointing sales of this jetliner caused Lockheed an agregate loss of US $2.5 billion.

L-1011-1 of Eastern Air Lines, the first company to operate the TriStar. Miami Airport, March 1984.

L-1011   Among the many production models of the Tri-Star the most representative was the L-1011-1, initially developed for short/medium range hauls. Subsequently, -100 and -200 series were added for increased range, followed by the -500 with a shortened fuselage to cater for a lesser number of passengers on long-distance routes. Deliveries of the L-1011-500s from factory inventory will continue till 1986.

L-1011-500 of Alia (The Royal Jordan Airlines) at Copenhagen Airport, July 1982.

Above left: *L-1011 of Air Portugal (TAP)*

Below left: *L-1011-1 of Trans World Airlines at Los Angeles Airport, August 1982.*
Above right: *L-1011-200 of Gulf Air, jointly owned by the four Gulf nations. Heathrow Airport, July 1982.*

Below right: *Saudi Arabia's flag carrier Saudia operates this L-1011-200. Heathrow Airport, September 1982.*

Airbus A300 (International)   A wide-bodied twin-jet developed by a consortium of European nations. After the Second World War, American-built passenger aircraft dominated the world's air transport leaving only a few European-evolved aircraft for firms to stay in business. The A300 is a product of cooperation between several European nations to regain the position on the market lost to the USA. The first Airbus took to the air in October 1972, and went into service in May 1974. At first, orders were slow in coming, and production progressed in the absence of a definitive schedule for delivery. However, the operating economics of the Airbus gradually won recognition and there are now more than 250 machines in service.

At present, the manufacture and assembly work is jointly undertaken by France, West Germany, UK and Spain, with component manufacture subcontracted to Holland and Belgium. The Airbus has been developed through several versions, such as the A300B2 for short-haul routes, the B4 with increased fuel capacity and range, and the C4 and F4 convertibles for passenger/freight operations.

While the A310 is an offshoot of the A300, development work continues under the project designation TA9 by stretching the A300-600 fuselage, TA11 powered by four turbofans for long-range operations and the TA12 for long-range routes with a pair of powerplants as at present.

The latest major production version A300-600 incorporates the rear fuselage developed for the A310, various internal improvements and a forward-facing two-man cockpit with CRT displays and new digital avionics.

Left: A 300B2 Airbus of Toa Domestic Airways taking off from the offshore airport of Nagasaki for Tokyo, November 1983.

Above left: A 300B4 of Eastern Air Lines, the first American operator to adopt the Airbus. Miami Airport, April 1984.

Above right: A 300B4 of Alitalia, Italy's flag carrier. Heathrow Airport, September 1984.

Below: A 300B4 of Air France, the first airline to place an order for the Airbus. Heathrow Airport, September 1984.

Airbus's own A300-600 airborne at the Farnborough Air Show, September 1984.

Airbus A310 (International)   A shorter-fuselage version of the A300 with advanced technology wings of shorter span and incorporating the latest of cockpit instrumentation to meet the expected future demands. The prototype first flew in April 1982, and was the first Airbus to feature the advanced two-man flight deck. Its medium-range variant A310-200 is to be followed by the -300 with extended range capability.

A310-200 of British Caledonian Airways at the Farnborough Air Show, September 1984.

19

Boeing 767 A twin-jet airliner developed for the 200-seater market, first flown in September 1981.

The appellation 'wide-bodied' is given to aircraft having a fuselage of swollen configuration compared to that of conventional airliners. The 767 ranks just midway between these two extremes and its fuselage is characterised by two aisles in the cabin for enhanced passenger comfort. Its modern cockpit is also a good selling point.

One of the unique features of the 767 is that both Japan and Italy participated in its development and production, their share amounting to 15 percent of the work each.

The original intention was to develop two versions, the 767-100 and the 767-200 'stretched' fuselage variant of the -100. However, with no orders received from airlines for the -100, the current production is concentrated on the -200 and its increased range variant, -200ER. Another version, the 767-300 with an even more 'stretched' fuselage to seat up to 330 passengers, is under development.

Left: *All Nippon Airways Boeing 767-200, which has a seating capacity of 236, at Osaka Airport, November 1983.*
Above: *Boeing 767-200 of Delta Air Lines based at Atlanta, Georgia. Miami Airport, March 1984.*

Boeing 767 Introduced as a medium-haul commercial transport, the 767 has grown to increase its range. On the ER version, the cruise distance is boosted to 7500 km (4000 nm), qualifying it for the trans-Atlantic service. Plans for a further increase in range are being considered by Boeing and thus the trend of changing twin-jet airliners into aircraft suitable for long-range operations, as exemplified by the A310-300, may well be accelerated.
Boeing 767-200 of Britannia Airways, a passenger/freight charter flight operator. Gatwick Airport, September 1984.

22

BAe/Aérospatiale Concorde (International)   After a protracted period of development since the prototype made its maiden flight in March 1968, the world's first supersonic airliner went into service in January 1976.
Despite the obvious technological innovation of the design, the uneconomical operation and the noise problem of this SST have proved detrimental for the Concorde and the production was terminated after only 16 examples were completed.
British Airways' Concorde. Farnborough Air Show, September 1980. The only other user of this SST is Air France.

Boeing 707/720 America's first turbojet airliner, the 707 was developed from the Boeing 367-87 prototype which first flew in 1954. Thanks to the revolutionary capabilities of this aircraft, achieving speed and payload performance almost double that of contemporary turboprop airliners, the Boeing 707 immediately gained the dominating position on the intercontinental and international routes. Its rival DC-8, appearing soon afterwards, failed in its attempts to catch up with the 707 and was destined to lag behind in the number of orders and years of production.

Production of the 707 civil transport terminated in 1982 after the completion of 962 aircraft, the world's highest output of four-engined commercial jets. In addition, 154 shorter-body intermediate range 720s were built, together with some 820 KC-135 flight-refuelling tankers and C-135 military transports. The appearance of the 747, DC-10 and L-1011 has contributed to the gradual withdrawal of the 707/720 from regular airline service to charter flights and freight transport. However, even these operations are affected by noise restriction rules, the consequence of which may well be that most of the 707/720s are destined soon to retire from the scene.

Left: *Boeing 707-320C of Libyan Arab Airlines. Heathrow Airport, September 1984.*

Above: *Boeing 720B of Conair of Scandinavia, a charter flight operator based in Copenhagen. Copenhagen Airport, July 1983.*

Below left: *Boeing 720B of Ecuador's flag carrier, Ecuatoriana, at Miami Airport, March 1984.*

Below right: *Air Zimbabwe's Boeing 707-320B at Gatwick Airport, September 1984.*

McDonnell Douglas DC-8 Proposed as a four-engined jetliner to compete with the Boeing 707, the DC-8 was launched in May 1958. During its production life the DC-8 design progressed from the -10 to -50 series and eventually the DC-8-60 'stretched'-body version developed in the mid-1960s to compete with other designs of that type. Production was terminated in 1972 after the completion of 556 aircraft.

The total number of DC-8s built was to remain only about half that of 707s, but the structural strength of the -60 series was noted by Commacorp which converted about 100 DC-8-60s into -70 series by re-engining the airframe with new turbofans intended to achieve higher performance and reduced noise levels. Although at this late stage plans also exist to modify the 707 into a reduced noise level passenger airliner, the fully modernised DC-8-70 may well gain the upper hand and remain operational longer than the Boeing 707.

Above: *DC-8-63CF of Arrow Air, one of the charter/freight service operators in the USA. Miami Airport, April 1984.*

Centre left: *DC-8-33 of Dominica's air freight specialist Aeromar. Miami Airport, March 1984.*

Centre right: *DC-8-62 of Rich International Airways, a Miami-based charter flight operator. Miami Airport, March 1984.*

Below left: *DC-8-73AF of United Parcel Service handling door-to-door delivery of small cargoes. Ontario Airport, August 1983.*

Below right: *DC-8F-55 of Surinam Airways. Miami Airport, March 1984.*

Left: *Delta Airlines DC-8-71. Re-engined with new type of jet engines of greater by-pass ratio, the aircraft became much quieter. Las Vegas Airport, April 1983.*

Ilyushin Il-62   The first Soviet four-jet long-range airliner, featuring rear-mounted powerplants similar to the BAe VC 10 in contrast to the contemporary Boeing 707 and DC-8 with underwing engines.
The first Soviet four-jet long-range airliner, with powerplants mounted in the rear similar to the British BAe VC 10, in contrast to the contemporary American

practice. The Il-62 entered regular service in 1967 and has remained in continuous production as the principal long-range airliner of the Communist block.

Tarom Rumanian Airlines Ilyushin Il-62M. Copenhagen Airport, July 1983.

Tupolev Tu-154 This rear-engined T-tail trijet for medium-range operations made its first flight in 1968. It resembles the Boeing 727 in outline but incorporates the traditional Tupolev design feature of retracting the main undercarriage into wing fairings. To date, some 600 Tu-154s have been registered.
Balkan Bulgarian Airlines Tupolev Tu-154B. Copenhagen Airport, July 1983.

Boeing 727 The best-selling jet airliner, with 1832 aircraft registered since it first flew in February 1963 to August 1984 when production terminated. Proposed as a rear-jet airliner for short/medium ranges, it shared this design concept with the British Trident, the development of which was already in progress. However, the 727 caught up with and surpassed the Trident by achieving higher efficiency thanks to the adoption of larger cross-section fuselage to increase passenger accommodation, combined with powerful high-lift systems. Boeing's success was assured by the timely development of the 727-200 series, a 'stretched'-body version of the 727-100 which, combined with the cost benefits of mass production, helped to confirm its leading position.

The original 727-100 airliner was complemented by other models, the -100C passenger/freight convertible variant and the -100QC quick-change freighter. Altogether, 572 examples of the -100 series were built before commencing the -200 series production.

Left: *Boeing 727-100C of Wien Air Alaska engaged in mixed passenger/cargo transport.*

Above: *Boeing 727-100C of Emery Worldwide, one of the leaders in airfreight pickup/delivery service. Seattle-Tacoma Airport, August 1982.*

Centre left: *Boeing 727-100C of Aviateca, Guatemala's flag carrier. Miami Airport, March 1984.*

Centre right: *Boeing 727-100 of T-Bird Air based at Houston, Texas. Las Vegas Airport, April 1983.*

Below left: *Boeing 727-100 of SAHSA (Serviceo Aereo de Honduras S.A.) of Honduras. Miami Airport, March 1984.*

Below right: *Alaska Airlines' Boeing 727-100, with an Eskimo head symbol on the tail fin. Seattle-Tacoma Airport, August 1982.*

Boeing 727   The three-engined 727-100 ushered in the age of jetliner service on the domestic air networks all over the world, but it soon had to give place to the -200 series with elongated fuselage to cope with the rapid growth in the number of air travellers. This 'stretched' version of the 727 with a seating capacity almost equal to that of the 707 was introduced on local and shorter international routes, and its operating economics soon attracted the attention of all airlines.

Formerly of Braniff Airways, this Boeing 727-200 is now used by Cayman Airways serving the British Cayman islands. Miami Airport, March 1984.

32

Boeing 727 Due to its increased passenger accommodation, the 727-200, completed in 1967, had shorter range than the -100 series. Four years later, the advanced 727-200 made its debut. Retaining the same overall configuration, this new version featured augmented fuel capacity and modernised cabin interior, paid for by increased all-up weight. The advanced 727-200 became so popular that Boeing's plans to develop a new 200-seat airliner were shelved since airlines were more interested in the low price of the advanced -200 than the improved operating economics of a new series.

Favoured as it was, the 727 too reached the end of its production life, and under the current more stringent noise controls this aircraft is now being gradually phased out.

1st row left: *Boeing 727-200 of Braniff Airways, USA. The airline ran into financial difficulties, was reorganised and is active again. Los Angeles Airport, March 1984.*

1st row right: *Boeing 727-200 of Continental Airlines. This airline is part of Air Texas. Las Vegas Airport, April 1983.*

2nd row left: *Air Jamaica's Boeing 727-200 with its humming bird symbol displayed on the tail fin. Miami Airport, July 1984.*

2nd row right: *Boeing 727-200 operated by LACSA of Costa Rica, Miami Airport, March 1984.*

3rd row left: *Boeing 727-200 of Sterling Airways, a Danish charter carrier operator. Copenhagen Airport, July 1983.*

3rd row right: *Syrian Arab Airlines Boeing 727-200. Copenhagen Airport, July 1983.*

4th row left: *Boeing 727-200 of Sun Country Airlines, one of the smaller air transport carriers based in Minneapolis, USA. Las Vegas Airport, April 1983.*

4th row right: *Boeing 727-223 of American Airlines.*

BAe Trident The epoch-making concept of a rear-engined trijet was first embodied in the design of Trident which competed with the Boeing 727. Though several versions were developed, the project closed after only 117 aircraft were built. A total of 35 Tridents were exported to China.

British Airways' Trident 2E, which has its nose wheel off-set to the left.

Yakovlev Yak-42   An enlarged version of the Yak-40, this three-engined passenger transport first flew in 1975 and commenced regular service in 1980. It was assumed at the time that the Yak-42 would be mass-produced to become the principal short-range Soviet airliner. However, the number built is still relatively small, due perhaps to some problems not yet resolved.

Aeroflot Yak-42 taking part in the Paris Air Show. Le Bourget Airport, June 1981.

Boeing 757 This twin-jet, developed for short-haul operations and seating slightly less passengers than the 767, made its first flight in February 1982. It is based on the 727 fuselage, but provided with new wings and shares the modern cockpit instrumentation introduced on the 767.

Initially, two versions were contemplated but since no orders were received for the shorter-body -100 series, production is concentrated on the -200 series. *Boeing 757-200 of Eastern Air Lines, USA. The large tailplane is most noticeable in this head-on view. Miami Airport, March 1984.*

Boeing 757 Boeing's ambition in placing the 757 as a successor to the 727-200 series included a sales target of 300 units in the first five years, thereby securing a firm place on the market. These hopes seem misplaced, as orders awarded so far barely cover 150 aircraft sold. At this rate it is unlikely that the 757 will ever join the fleet of bestsellers.

British Airways' Boeing 757-200. Each 757 of BA's fleet is named after a castle. Heathrow Airport, September 1984.

37

Boeing 737   This small short-haul twin-jet airliner was Boeing's response to the jet age on the local air transport market. The 737 first flew in April 1967 and went into regular service in February 1968. In this class, the BAC 111 and DC-9 had already been paving the way but the 737 offered a definite feature distinct from its rivals, in that the stout fuselage of the same cross-section as that of the 727 was combined with wings fitted with powerful high-lift devices, with the jet engines faired underneath.

The first 737 version was the 115-seat -100 series, which was discontinued after just 30 aircraft. Production then focused on the -200 series, a 'stretched' fuselage version, which was followed by the advanced 737-200 incorporating many detail improvements, rather than commencing production of the -300 series which would have required a major modification of the fuselage. The direction taken by Boeing contrasts noticeably from that of the DC-9 which came in many 'stretched' versions. Orders received for the Boeing 737-100/-200 series have reached well over 1200, and as the new 737-300 series also fares well, it is quite possible that a new best-selling commercial aircraft record will be established by the 737 jointly with the DC-9.

Left: *Boeing 737-200 of Aloha Airlines which links the islands of Hawaii. Kahului Airport, Maui, April 1982.*

Above left: *Air France Boeing 737-200 at Copenhagen Airport, April 1982.*

Above right: *Boeing 737-200 of Piedmont Airlines which serves the local network along the East Coast of the USA. Washington National Airport, November 1981.*

Centre left: *Boeing 737-200 of Southwest Airlines flying over Okinawa Naha Airport.*

Centre right: *Lufthansa Boeing 737-200. This West German flag carrier was the first to order the Boeing 737, initially the -100 series. Copenhagen Airport, July 1983.*

Below left: *Boeing 737-200 of Spantax, a Spanish charter flight operator. Gatwick Airport, September 1984.*

Below right: *Boeing 737-200 of Orion Airways, a British company. Gatwick Airport, September 1984.*

Boeing 737 For many years the 737 production was limited to the advanced -200 series and its passenger/freight convertible -200C variant, but a new model was finally added in the 1980s. Known as 737-300, it was designed to have the 'stretched' body of the 737-200 series seating 121–147 passengers and powered by a new type of engine, the aim being to fill the gap between the 737-200 and the 757-200. The new Boeing first flew in March 1984, and already over 150 orders have been received.

Studies are continually in progress on several new variants, including the -100L, a re-engined shorter-body 100-seater, and the -400 series, a further 'stretched'-body 150-seater. Such trends led to an intensified competition between the 737 and the DC-9 as McDonnell Douglas, through several 'stretched' versions, now have the MD-80 in the 150-seater class. Decision has also been reached regarding the development of the shorter-fuselage MD-87 and planning of the longer-fuselage MD-89.

The 737 has a six-row seat arrangement in its wide body and the powerplants mounted under the wings, while the DC-9/MD-80 has a five-row layout of seats and is rear-engined. It should be interesting to see where the rivalry of these two contrasting design concepts will lead.

Above: *Boeing 737-200 of American West, one of the operators which mushroomed after the deregulation of air transport in the USA. Los Angeles Airport, March 1984.*

Below left: *Boeing 737-200 of Air Cal which operates over California. Los Angeles Airport, August 1982.*

Below right: *Boeing 737-200 of Air Europe, a British charter carrier operator. Gatwick Airport, September 1984.*

Right: *US Air's Boeing 737-300, which participated in the Farnborough Air Show, during a test flight in September 1984.*

McDonnell Douglas DC-9 As a rule, some time after its appearance a passenger aircraft goes through the process of 'jumboising' the airframe by means of 'stretching' the fuselage in order to respond to the airline demands for increased accommodation. The DC-9 is an exception however in that it has successfully grown through frequent 'stretch' operations.

The initial DC-9-10 series with a standard seating of 80 was followed by the -30 series (105 seats), then the -40 series (115 seats), the -50 series (125 seats), and by the time the -80 series (145 seats; later re-designated MD-80) appeared the airframe length had grown by 13.23 m (43 ft 2 in) and the passenger capacity increased by 80 percent.

During this process, the DC-9's span was slightly extended for the -30 series, then the wing surfaces enlarged for the -80 series, which was also fitted with improved powerplants of higher output and lower noise level. Such development was only possible because of the sound engineering of the original DC-9 design.

Left: *DC-9-41 of SAS Scandinavian Airlines System jointly operated by the three countries of that region. Copenhagen Airport, July 1983.*

Above left: *DC-9-15F of Emerald Air, USA. The initial -10 series was designed for freight service, but this particular aircraft carries passengers. Dallas/Fort Worth Airport, July 1982.*

Above right: *DC-9-14 of Sun World, a new airline activated in 1983. Oklahoma City Airport, April 1984.*

Centre left: *New York Air's DC-9-32. Washington National Airport, November 1981.*

Centre right: *DC-9-31 of Ozark Air Lines which covers the midwestern part of the USA. Miami Airport, March 1984.*

Below left: *DC-9-51 of BWIA International Trinidad and Tobago Airways. Miami Airport, March 1984.*

Below right: *JAT Yugoslav Airlines DC-9-32. Yugoslavia belongs to the Eastern bloc but employs almost exclusively American civil transport aircraft. Copenhagen Airport, July 1983.*

DC-9 Through repeated 'stretch' efforts the DC-9 evolved into an advanced model, the MD-80 (DC-9-80), practically leaving the lower passenger capacity airliner market to the Boeing 737. As a result, McDonnell Douglas decided in January 1985 on the MD-87 project, a shorter-fuselage development of the current MD-80 series (MD-81 and -82 with different gross weights, and the MD-83 with increased range). Plans have also been revealed for expanding the DC-9 family by an additional project known as the MD-89 which will be the ultimate of the 'stretched'-fuselage DC-9s. Although the design of the aircraft will incorporate the latest state-of-art technology it may have to sacrifice some operating economics. McDonnell Douglas believe that the low scale price attained by large-scale production of the MD-80 series with a high commonality of components, should be an incentive for airlines to place orders.

The total DC-9 production embracing -10 to -50 series amounts to 976 aircraft, while orders for the MD-80 series have already exceeded 350. By how many units this figure will increase in the future deserves attention.

Above: Austrian Airlines MD-81. This Austrian airline has also ordered the MD-87. Heathrow Airport, September 1984.

Centre left: MD-81 of Pacific Southwest Airlines operating over California. Los Angeles Airport, August 1982.

Centre right: Aeromexico MD-82 at Miami Airport, May 1982.

Below left: MD-81 of Hawaiian Air. Its vertical fin displays a Hawaiian girl's profile and a hibiscus flower to accentuate the tropical theme. Honolulu Airport, March 1982.

Below right: MD-81 of Toa Domestic Airlines taking off from Kagoshima Airport with Mt. Kirishima in the background, November 1983.

Right: MD-82 of Muse Air, USA, its logo painted in impressive script. Yuma Airport, July 1982.

BAe 111 Developed two years ahead of its rivals, the BAe One-Eleven twin-engined short-haul jetliner was eventually overwhelmed by the DC-9 and Boeing 737, and production terminated after 232 aircraft. More recently, the One-Eleven has been revived in Romania, the licence-built aircraft being known as Rombac III.

BAe One-Eleven Series 475 of Pacific Express, USA. Los Angeles Airport, August 1982.

Tupolev Tu-134   A derivative of early Soviet jet-powered passenger aircraft evolved from bomber designs, this short-range twin-jet commercial transport displays modern styling with powerplants mounted in the rear and a T-tail. The type entered scheduled service in 1966, and some 600 TU-134s are reported to have been built.

LOT-Polish Airlines Tu-134A. The bomber-style nose panel is used by the navigator. Heathrow Airport, September 1984.

Fokker F28 Fellowship   A twin-jet commercial transport developed to serve the local network, the F28 Fellowship is smaller than the initial version of the DC-9. Determined sales efforts have resulted in the cumulative orders for over 200 aircraft. At present a completely new 'stretched' fuselage design powered by two turbofan engines and known as Fokker 100 is under development.

Fokker F28 Mk 4000 of Linjeflyg serving the domestic network in Sweden, at Copenhagen Airport.

Aérospatiale Caravelle   The world's first short/medium-haul jet airliner, the Caravelle is also famous for being the first to be powered by rear-mounted engines. First flown in 1955, a total of 282 Caravelles were completed before the production came to a halt in 1972. Only a few Caravelles are still in service.

Caravelle 10R of CTA, a subsidiary of Swiss Air. Gatwick Airport, September 1984.

49

BAe 146 The only jetliner of shoulder-wing layout, the BAe 146 is powered by four small engines to serve the local network. It offers wide-body standard of comfort in the arrangement of six seats across the cabin. The first flight was recorded in September 1981. At present, the initial 146-100 design and the 146-200, a 'stretched'-body version of the -100, are in parallel production.

Airlines of Western Australia BAe 146-200 at Farnborough Air Show, September 1984.

BAe 146 The BAe 146's principal selling points are that it is quieter than its immediate competitor Fokker F28, and that the -100 series offers better airfield performance while the 146-200 series can carry more passengers. However, sales to date are unsatisfactory, and the 146-300 series with an even longer fuselage seating up to 130 passengers is now under development.

Air Wisconsin's BAe 146-200, the first aircraft of this type exported to the USA. Farnborough Air Show, September 1982.

de Havilland Canada Dash 7 This 50-seat turboprop is noted for its excellent STOL performance attained by means of large-surface flaps designed to retain most of the propeller airstream by the wings. It is extremely quiet, with the engine exhausts pointing upwards and its large-diameter propellers rotating at slow speed.

Maersk Air's Dash 7 which serves the domestic routes in Denmark. Copenhagen Airport, July 1983.

DHC Dash 7 First flown in March 1975, the Dash 7 went into regular service in 1978. Its fuselage size is comparable to the Fokker F27 and BAe 748, but few airlines are inclined to attach importance to the STOL features of the Dash 7. Consequently, the total number of Dash 7s built to date is relatively small, just over 100 aircraft.

Dash 7 of Brymon Airways of UK approaching Heathrow Airport at dusk, September 1984.

Lockheed L-188 Electra   The only large American medium-range
four-turboprop airliner, the L-188 Electra was first flown in December 1957. It
was sold on the advocated feature of speed, much faster than contemporary
piston-engined aircraft, but the L-188 was soon to be superseded by the
medium-range jetliner and production ceased after only 170 aircraft were built.
The remaining Electras are mainly operated as freight-carrying transports.
*Lockheed L-188AF serving as a freight carrier by TACA of El Salvador. Miami
Airport, March 1984.*

Ilyushin Il-18 Following its first flight in 1957, this four turboprop-powered airliner was produced in large numbers and eventually formed a fleet of over 700 in regular service with Aeroflot and other Eastern European airlines on domestic trunk routes as well as medium-range international routes. Some Il-18s still remain in service.

Ilyushin Il-18V of TAROM Romanian Air Transport. This particular aircraft was built in 1961. Copenhagen Airport, July 1983.

55

Fokker F27 Friendship   This twin turboprop has been in continuous production since the prototype made its first flight in 1955, and the total orders exceed 750 aircraft. A follow-on development known as Fokker 50 powered by new technology engines driving six-bladed propellers is in progress, and the new aircraft is scheduled to commence commercial service in 1986.

Fokker F27 of Horizon Air, USA, at Seattle Tacoma Airport, August 1982. This aircraft was built under licence in the USA.

Handley Page Herald The prototype of this feederliner was completed with four piston engines, but later redesigned as a twin turboprop. In the event, the Herald was overshadowed by the Fokker F27, and only 50 were built. A few Heralds are still in use.

Herald 200 of Air UK, one of the few aircraft of this type still remaining in service. Heathrow Airport, July 1983.

BAe 748 Proposed as a DC-3 replacement as was the Fokker F27, this twin turboprop feederliner first flew in 1960 and is still in production. Including those built under licence in India, more than 400 748s have been put into service. Unlike the F27 however, the 748 is of low-wing layout similar to the Japanese YS-11, though smaller in size.

Bahamas Air BAe 748 Series 2A which operates between the islands of that region. Miami Airport, March 1984.

BAe 748   The current version of the 748 is Series 2B which has wings of wider chord compared to the earlier aircraft. An advanced model known as ATP with new powerplants and a 'stretched' fuselage to seat 64 passengers is under development.

BAe 748 Series 2B of Air Virginia, a commuter carrier operator, at the Washington National Airport, November 1981.

NAMC YS-11 Japan's first postwar airliner, the YS-11 was the product of a joint undertaking by several private Japanese companies with government participation known as Nippon Aircraft Mfg Co. First flown in August 1962, the basic 60-passenger production version entered service in April 1965. Forming the main equipment then used on domestic Japanese routes, the YS-11 was notably larger than the Fokker F27 and BAe 748, and possessed outstanding STOL characteristics. A number of YS-11s were exported to the USA, Canada and several South American countries.

Although a successful design, particularly as the first turboprop airliner ever built in Japan, the YS-11 became commercially unviable due to poor sales promotion and lack of fund procurement, reaching the stage where each aircraft built contributed to the accumulated losses. As a result, only 180 aircraft were completed before the production was halted in 1973.

As an aircraft, the YS-11 was always favoured by airlines and some are still in service on minor local routes. It is also a popular aircraft on the second-hand market, particularly in the USA. The YS-11 could have been a long-seller like the Fokker F27 if the company was given a chance to restructure for continued production.

Left: YS-11A-500 of PBA (Provincetown Boston Airways) at Miami Airport, March 1984.

Above: YS-11A-600 of Mid-Pacific Airlines which serves the Hawaiian islands. Kahului Airport, April 1982.

Below left: YS-11A-200 of Southwest Air Lines, a regional operator serving the Okinawan Islands. Naha Airport, November 1983.

Below right: YS-11-100 of Nihon Kinkyori Airways serving the remote locations of Japan. Iki Airport, November 1983.

Shorts 330/360   A light twin-turboprop regional air service transport with a standard seating for 30 passengers, the Shorts 330 was evolved from the Skyvan before any other country had started development work on large commuter class aircraft. First flown in August 1974, the Shorts 330 went into regular service two years later.

The 330 is conspicuous for its utility styling, with the square-section fuselage based on the Skyvan. It is not very fast, and the unpressurised cabin lacks comfort, but the 330 is nevertheless a commercial success due to its safe-life concept and by being the first in the large commuter market.

Three versions are now available: the 330-200 standard passenger carrier, the 330-UTT military utility tactical transport, and the Sherpa freighter version of the 330-200.

The Shorts 360 is a 'stretched' development of the 330 seating 36 passengers and incorporating strengthened outer wing panels, a new tail unit and more powerful engines. It made its aerial debut in June 1981, with the first production aircraft following in August 1982.

Developed specifically for short-haul airline operations, the 360 was an immediate success and the total orders and options now stand at over 90 aircraft. Even when the commuter airliner has become more practical than novel, its low price and operating economics remain attractive selling points. It is interesting to see how much longer this trend will continue.

Left: *Shorts 360 of Suburban Airlines, USA, and Shorts 330-200 of Genair, UK, during a formation flight at the Farnborough Air Show, September 1982.*

Above: *Shorts 330 of British Midland Airways. Heathrow Airport, July 1983.*

Below left: *Shorts 360 of Airbusiness, a Danish commuter/charter transport company. Farnborough Air Show, September 1984.*

Below right: *Shorts 360 of Imperial Airline, USA. Los Angeles Airport, April 1984.*

Saab Fairchild 340 (International)   This 30-seat twin-turboprop transport is the first collaborative effort of this kind between European and American aerospace industries. Of elegant low-wing layout, the 340 was designed with emphasis on simplicity of systems, operation and maintenance. It is the first aircraft in the new generation 30-seater class, featuring a pressurised cabin.

First flown in prototype form in January 1981, the 340 was approved for passenger carrying and entered service in May 1984.

Saab Fairchild 340 on a demonstration flight at the Farnborough Air Show, September 1984.

de Havilland Canada Dash 8   This twin-turboprop short-haul transport in the 30/40 seat category made its first flight in October 1984. With emphasis on fuel efficiency and quiet operations, the Dash 8 also excels in STOL performance compared to other aircraft in its class. The relatively wide body allows four seats abreast, and the Dash 8 is being offered in two basic versions, as a commuter for local air services and a corporate with extended range capability for operations in North America.

Dash 8 with landing gear retracted after take off at the Farnborough Air Show, September 1984.

65

Aérospatiale/Aeritalia ATR 42 (International)   The largest of all new generation commuters, the twin-turboprop ATR 42 is a joint French/Italian development. First flown in August 1984, the ATR 42 incorporates a number of advanced technological features combined with excellent flight performance. Already the initial version has passenger capacity equal to that of the Fokker F27 and BAe 748, and plans are in hand to 'stretch' the fuselage to accommodate 58/62 passengers. Other projects include all-freight and military versions.

The ATR 42 development aircraft under test at the Aérospatiale Toulouse plant.

EMBRAER EMB-120 Brasilia   Following their success with the Bandeirante, the EMBRAER company evolved the EMB-120 light twin-turboprop passenger and cargo transport. First flown in July 1983, it is not only the smallest of all new 30-seater commuters but also the most cost-competitive. Options on more than 110 Brasilias (including 26 for the air forces of Brazil and Chile) were in hand by mid-1984.
The second EMB-120 prototype in metallic finish coming in to land at the Farnborough Air Show, September 1984.

67

Airtech CN-235 (International) This twin-turboprop commuter and utility transport is the joint product of CASA of Spain and Nurtanio of Indonesia, and one prototype was built and completed simultaneously late in 1983 in each country. The CN-235 has been optimised for short-haul operations and the design is notable for its rear cargo door. By March 1984 the Airtech had 110 firm orders for the CN-235.

The first CN-235 built in Spain during a demonstration flight at the Farnborough Air Show in September 1984.

Dornier Do 228   An unpressurised twin-turboprop commuter and utility transport, first flown in March 1981. This design is notable for its uniquely-shaped lifting surfaces known as High Technology Wings. Production began early in 1982, and five versions are available at present, including two 'stretched' fuselage variants seating 19 passengers. By spring 1984 Dornier had over 100 firm orders and options in hand, and licence-manufacturing rights had been negotiated with HAL in India.

Do 228-200 operated by Japan Air Commuter, a subsidiary of Toa Domestic Airways, at Tokunoshima Airport in April 1983.

69

EMBRAER EMB-110 Bandeirante In the smaller twin-engined commuter/general purpose transport class the Brazilian EMB-110 is second only to the Canadian DHC-6 Twin Otter. To date, almost 450 Bandeirantes of various versions have been delivered to 80 civil and military operators in 26 countries, and more orders are in hand. Variants built include cargo and passenger transports, utility and paradropping, and search and rescue. A maritime surveillance version development is known as EMB-111.

EMB-110 P1 of Royal Airlines, one of a considerable number of Bandeirantes exported to the USA.

de Havilland DHC-6 Twin Otter   Designed to achieve a high degree of utility and STOL performance, the Twin Otter has become the most popular commuter aircraft in the world. Since its first flight in 1965, more than 810 of this light twin-turboprop transport have been delivered to civil and military customers in 74 countries.

DHC-6-200 operated by West Air Commuter Airlines of California at Monterey Airport in August 1983.

71

CASA C-212 Aviocar   As evidenced by the rear cargo handling door, this twin-turboprop STOL utility transport was designed with an eye on the military market, and by early 1984 nearly 350 Aviocars had been delivered, about half of them to military customers. Another point in Aviocar's favour is its attractive price.

Air Florida commuter CASA 212 at Miami Airport in March 1984.

IAI Arava Twin-turboprop STOL civil/military transport, evolved from the initial IAI 101 of 1972, which was not produced. At present available in four versions: as IAI 201 civil transport, IAI 201 for general military duties, IAI 202 modified transport with winglets and longer fuselage, and updated IAI 101B passenger/cargo variant mainly for the US market (where sold as Cargo Commuterliner).
California's Airspur used to operate the IAI 101B for small cargo deliveries. Los Angeles Airport, August 1982.

GAF Nomad   This simple twin-turboprop STOL transport was developed by the Australian Government Aircraft Factory (GAF) with emphasis on utility, STOL performance and low cost. First flown in 1971, the Nomad was built in two versions, N22 and N24, both for civil and military use. The total production amounted to 17 aircraft.

N24A of Nagasaki Airways serving the remote island routes, photographed at Iki Airport in November 1983.

BAe Jetstream   Originally a Handley Page design, modified and updated by BAe. First flown in March 1980, the Jetstream 31 is now available in six versions, including Commuter, Corporate, Executive Shuttle and military.

Early Jetstream Mk I of Apollo Airways (now Pacific Coast Airlines) at Los Angeles Airport in August 1982.

Fairchild Metro   This 20-seat commuter airliner has some exceptional features for its class, such as a pressure cabin and relatively high speed. The fuselage is impressively slender, but seating only two abreast. The executive transport version for 12/15 passengers is designated Merlin IV.

Air South's Metro, Miami Airport, August 1982.

Beech C99 Airliner Originally known as Commuter 99, the design of this 15-seat airliner is based on the King Air 90 executive transport. It has a non-pressurised cabin with a hatch in the lower rear fuselage for a ground cargo pack.

An enlarged pressurised cabin development, first flown in September 1982, is designated Beech 1900.

Wings West Beech C99 serving the West coast of the USA. Los Angeles Airport, August 1982.

Grumman G-73 Mallard   Mallard is an amphibian passenger transport, 61 of which were built between 1946 and 1951. At a later stage, the powerplants were changed from piston engines to turboprops, improving the flight performance and operating economics.

Left: *Turbo Mallard of Chalk's International Airline flying from Miami Watson Island to the Caribbean islands, March 1984.*

Convair 440   The twin-engined Convair 240, 340 and 440 series were the fast-selling successors to the Douglas DC-3/C-47, the principal transport aircraft of postwar days. The later modified versions with turboprop engines are known as Convair 580, 600 and 640.

Above left: Key Airlines Convair 440 engaged in passenger transport to Las Vegas. Las Vegas Airport, April 1983.

Douglas DC-6   This large piston-engined airliner played a big role in postwar civil aviation. Built to compete with the Lockheed Constellation, the initial DC-6 airliners were followed by DC-6A windowless freighters and then the 54/102-passenger DC-6B, growing into the largest four-engined airliner family of those days.

Above right: *West Germany's DHL Cargo DC-6A freighter in Honolulu, Hawaii, May 1982.*

Douglas DC-3   The most outstanding transport aircraft of the last half century, with well over 10,000 built since its first flight in 1935. During the Second World War, the simplified C-47 military version was produced in very large series, and today the ubiquitous Dakota can still be seen flying on a variety of transport tasks all over the world.

Right: *DC-3 of a parachute club at Lodi Airport, California, August 1983.*